NGLÉS PARA NIÑOS

READ ENGLISH WITH ZIGZAG -3

ISBN: 978-1-914911-15-6

www.zigzagenglish.co.uk

ZIGZAG ENGLISH

OUR BOOKS FOR CHILDREN
www.zigzagenglish.co.uk

Our bilingual books for young children. *Funny stories in simple, useful everyday English, with colour photos.*
English with Tony -1- Tony moves house
English with Tony -2- Tony is happy
English with Tony -3- Tony's Christmas
English with Tony -4- Tony's holiday
My Best Friend

Our coursebook for child beginners *(age 7 to 11)*
English for Children - 1st Coursebook (Essential vocabulary and grammar for beginners)

Our series of dialogue books for beginners *(for beginners aged 7 - 11). With word lists, comprehension questions, speaking tasks and more.*
I Speak English Too! - 1
I Speak English Too! - 2

Our series of reading and comprehension books for beginners *(for beginners aged 7 - 11). With word lists, comprehension questions and more.*
Read English with Zigzag - 1
Read English with Zigzag - 2
Read English with Zigzag - 3
Read English with Zigzag 1, 2 and 3
      Audiobook - Books 1 + 2 (Audible)

The Learn English Activity Book for Children *(A1 - A2, elementary). (Recommended for children in early secondary school.)*

Our series of reading and comprehension books for children at elementary level *(recommended for ages 10 - 13). With word lists, comprehension and discussion questions and lots of language activities.*
Read English with Ben - 1
Read English with Ben - 2
Read English with Ben – 3

Our series of reading and discussion books (with writing tasks) for children at secondary school, A2 - B1
I Live in a Castle – Book 1 – The Choice
I Live in a Castle – Book 2 – The New Me

The Speak English, Read English, Write English Activity Books – *3 books from A1 to B2, for older children and adults.*

Our non-fiction book with language activities
Learn English with Fun Facts! – A2 – B2

English Dialogues for Secondary School – for ages 11 to 17, A2 – B2

OUR BOOKS FOR ADULTS

Our 3 Grammar books with grammar-focused dialogues
Learn English Grammar through Conversation – A1, A2 and B1

Our Dialogue books for adults (with vocabulary lists and comprehension questions)
50 very Easy Everyday English Dialogues (A2)
50 Easy Everyday English Dialogues (A2 - B1)
50 Intermediate Everyday English Dialogues (B1 - B2)
50 more Intermediate Everyday English Dialogues (B1 - B2)
40 Advanced Everyday English Dialogues (B2 – C1)
40 Intermediate Business English Dialogues (B1 - B2)
40 Advanced Business English Dialogues (B2 - C1)

Our activity books for adults and older children
The Speak English, Read English, Write English Activity Books – 3 books, for A1 - A2, A2 - B1 and B1 – B2.

Our non-fiction book with language activities
Learn English with Fun Facts! – A2 – B2

Contents

Los objetivos de esta serie de libros son:

1. Ofrecer una lectura divertida y amena.
2. Dotar a su hijo la confianza necesaria para leer en inglés.
3. Enseñar a su hijo palabras y frases clave. Los libros introducen, repiten y construyen sobre ellas poco a poco, para ampliar la comprensión del inglés de su hijo.
4. Ayudar a su hijo a aprender la gramática básica del inglés de forma sencilla.

Cómo utilizar esta serie de libros:

1. Tal vez su hijo disfrute leyendo los libros por su cuenta. ¡Estupendo! No obstante, si usted habla inglés, anímele a leer algunos capítulos en voz alta para ayudarle a mejorar su pronunciación. Hay disponible **un audiolibro de los dos primeros libros de Zigzag**.
2. Hay listas de vocabulario a lo largo de cada libro, que puede utilizar para ayudar a su hijo a aprender las palabras nuevas.
3. Encontrará preguntas de comprensión, con sus respectivas respuestas al final de cada libro. Por supuesto puede añadir más preguntas y conversar sobre la historia y los personajes.
4. Los libros incluyen actividades de aprendizaje para ayudar a su hijo con el vocabulario y la gramática.

Qué más? ¿Y ahora qué?

1. Nuestra serie de diálogos sencillos - I Speak English Too! - está pensada para aquellos padres que quieran ayudar a sus hijos a empezar a hablar inglés. Es ideal para que padres e hijos, o bien sólo los niños lean juntos. Empiece por lo más básico, introduciendo y ampliando las palabras y frases clave para ayudar a su hijo a progresar rápidamente. En pocas y divertidas lecciones, su hijo será capaz de mantener pequeñas conversaciones en inglés con usted.
2. La lectura de libros en inglés -por muy sencillos que sean- marca una gran diferencia. También recomendamos ver series de televisión sencillas para niños. Los audiolibros también son estupendos, sobre todo antes de acostarse (pues esto ayuda a retener el nuevo idioma). No espere que su hijo lo entienda todo en seguida: los audiolibros pueden escucharse una y otra vez, y su hijo entenderá más cada vez.

From wolf to pet

1 I'm not a cat

Oh, look at all those children. Hello, children! I'm your friend! Can I **wash** your **face** for you? Is that okay? Can we go for a walk? Can I take my ball? Can you **throw** the ball for me?

What's that? What did you say?

I'm not Zigzag, no. I'm not a cat. I'm not a tiger. Do I look like a cat or a tiger?

No, I don't. I look like a dog. That's because I AM A DOG.

I'm a beautiful, big, black and white dog. I'm white with black spots. I'm a dalmatian dog.

Do you know my name? Do you remember who I am?

That's right. I'm Pam!

Vocabulary:
- to wash   lavar
- face   cara
- to throw   lanzar

2 One or two things you need to know

If you have a dog:

1. You have to take your dog for a walk every morning.

2. You have to take your dog for a walk every evening.

3. Do NOT **forget** to take your dog for a walk!

Vocabulary:
- to forget   olvidar

3 Dogs are better than cats

I'm Pam. I'm not Zigzag, I'm Pam.

Sorry about that.

No, I'm not sorry. I'm not sorry - I'm **happy**. I'm happy, because - guess what? I'm **better** than Zigzag.

I'm a dog, and Zigzag is a cat. Zigzag is NOT A TIGER. He's a cat.

Dogs are better than cats. So - I'm better than Zigzag. **Right?**

I'm bigger than Zigzag. I'm nicer than Zigzag. I'm more beautiful than Zigzag. I'm more intelligent than Zigzag. I like children more than Zigzag does.

And this is my book. It's not Zigzag's book - it's mine!

Vocabulary:
- happy   feliz
- better   mejor
- right?   ¿verdad?

4 Big, bigger, biggest

This is a small dog. It's not very big. It's the smallest dog.

This is a bigger dog. It's quite big.

This dog is even bigger. It's the biggest dog. It's really very big. It's enormous.

5 A long time ago

Some dogs are big and some dogs are small. Some dogs have long **ears** and some dogs have short **tails**. Some dogs are brown and some dogs are white with black spots **like** me.

Some dogs...

Okay, you know what I mean. All dogs are **different**.

But a very, very, very, very, very long time ago, all dogs were the same. That's right - all dogs were:

WOLVES!!

Wolves are enormous. Wolves have **sharp teeth**. Wolves are really scary. But most of all, wolves are **BRAVE**.

A long time ago, I was a wolf. Now, I'm a dog and I live in Adam and Poppy's house with Zigzag the cat.

But I'm still brave.

Vocabulary:
- a long time ago   hace mucho tiempo
- ear   oreja
- tail   cola
- like   como
- different   diferente
- wolf   lobo
- sharp   agudo
- tooth   diente
- brave   valiente

6 Old enough

Adam is four years **younger** than Poppy. When Adam was a **baby**, Poppy was **already** at school. When Adam **learned** to talk, Poppy learned to read. When Adam learned to walk, Poppy learned to run races.

Then Adam went to nursery with the other very small children and **painted** pictures with his hands. And Poppy started to **write stories**.

But now, **at last**, Adam's old enough to go to school with Poppy.

On his first day at school, Adam was excited. He really wanted to go to school. He didn't want to be little. He wanted to be a big boy.

He walked to school with Mum and with Poppy and her best friend Jessica. He wore his **own** school uniform – black trousers and a red top. He had his own red book bag. He felt **proud**. He **felt** a little bit scared.

Questions:
1. *How much older than Adam is Poppy?*
2. *How did Adam feel about starting school?*
3. *Why was his book bag red?*

Vocabulary:
- younger   más joven
- baby   bebé
- already   ya
- to learn   aprender

- to paint   pintar
- to write   escribir
- story   cuento
- at last   por fin
- own   propio
- proud   orgulloso
- to feel   sentirse

7 A very brave thing

This summer, I did a very brave thing. I did the bravest thing a dog can do.

We all went for a picnic. Well, not Zigzag, because he's a cat. Cats have to stay at home.

There was a river. Mum and Dad and Poppy and I can swim. But Adam can't swim. He's too young.

Adam was in **danger**. Mum and Dad and Poppy were there. But they didn't **see** the danger.

I saw the danger. I saw Adam run and fall into the water. I jumped into the water. It was **deep**. It was too deep for me.

I swam to Adam. He put his **arms** round my **neck**. I **pulled** him out of the water.

Everyone said "Good dog! Brave dog!"

I'm a big, strong, brave dog and I **saved** Adam.

Vocabulary:
- danger   peligro

- to see   ver
- to fall   caer
- deep   profundo
- arm   brazzo
- neck   cuello
- to pull   tirar
- to save   salvar

8 At school

At school, there were so many children. There were hundreds of them. **Nearly all** of them were older and bigger than Adam. Because it was Adam's first day, Mum was there. She took a photo of Adam in front of the school. And then she went into the classroom with Adam. Adam wanted Mum to stay with him. He started to **cry**. But Mum said goodbye, and she **left**.

Adam looked at all the other boys and girls in his class. There were lots and lots of them. He **only** knew one of them. Billy, from nursery. Adam didn't like Billy, and Billy didn't like Adam. "Hello, Billy," said Adam. Billy said **nothing**.

Adam sat on the **floor** with all the other children. The teacher told a story. It was the story of Goldilocks and the Three Bears.

Questions:
1. *Why did mum go into the classroom with Adam?*
2. *Was Adam happy to be at school?*
3. *Why didn't Billy talk to Adam?*

Vocabulary:
- nearly   casi
- all   todos
- to cry   llorar
- to leave   irse
- only   sólo
- nothing   nada
- floor   suelo

9 Something interesting

Adam went to school today. It was very quiet here without him.

Mum and dad **were out**. Poppy and Adam were at school. Only Zigzag was here. I like Zigzag, but he's **just** a cat. He doesn't understand much. He went to school with Poppy once, but **I don't think he learned anything**.

I went into the garden. I watched Zigzag **catch** a spider. I watched Zigzag eat the spider. Zigzag said it was delicious. I looked for a spider, but I couldn't find one.

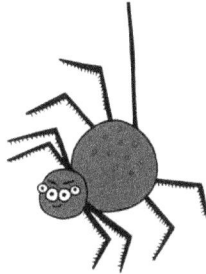

Then I saw something interesting. Something very interesting. The next door neighbour's white cat was in the next door neighbour's garden.

I did a bad thing. I knew it was a bad thing, but I did it.

I **barked** at the cat – WOOF WOOF! Then I jumped over the **fence** into the next door neighbour's garden. The cat ran. I chased her. I chased her round and round the garden and up the neighbour's tree. She sat in the tree and looked at me.

Vocabulary:
- were out   habían salido
- just   sólo
- he didn't learn anything   no aprendió nada
- to catch   atrapar
- to bark   ladrar
- fence   valla

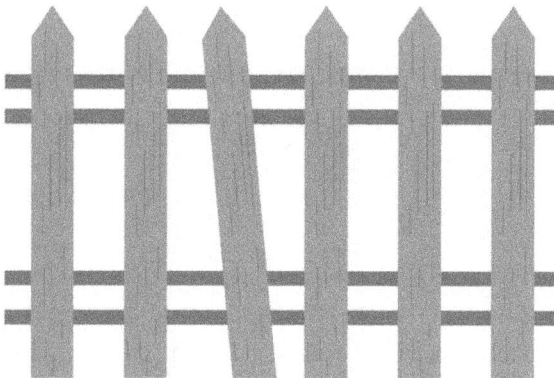

10 Goldilocks and the 3 bears

Goldilocks was a girl with **gold** hair (really?) who went into the **forest**, looking for some breakfast.

She found it in a bears' house (do bears live in houses?) and ate it.

Luckily for Goldilocks, the bears were out. Bears are extremely big and strong and sometimes eat little girls.

Then Goldilocks sat on a little chair and **broke** it.

She was tired, so she went upstairs to the bedroom and went to sleep on Baby Bear's bed.

When the three bears **got back** home, they were hungry. They wanted to eat their breakfast, but it was gone. Baby Bear wanted to sit on his chair, but it was broken. When they found Goldilocks on Baby Bear's bed, Father Bear wanted to eat her, but Baby Bear wanted to play with her.

Goldilocks **woke up**. She was scared. She jumped out of the window and ran home. She never went into the forest again.

Questions:
1. *Why did Goldilocks go into the forest?*
2. *Were the bears at home?*
3. *Did Baby Bear want to eat Goldilocks?*

Vocabulary:

- gold   dorado
- forest   bosque
- to break   romper
- to get back   volver
- to wake up   despertarse

11 Cat in a tree

The white cat sat in the tree. It sat in the tree for five long minutes.

I wanted that cat. I don't know why I wanted her, but I did.

Zigzag is a cat, and I don't chase Zigzag. But Zigzag is family. I chase every other cat. All dogs chase cats. It's what we do.

But I had a problem. Cats can **climb** trees. Dogs can't climb trees. The white cat was in a tree. I needed to **go up**, or I needed the cat to **come down**.

I tried to climb the tree. I really, really **tried**. But it was no good. I'm big, strong, brave and intelligent, but I can't climb.

I **asked** the cat to come down. I said I wanted to talk to her. I was very **polite**. She was polite too, but she said no. She didn't want to come down. She was comfortable in the tree. It was nice up there.

I wanted that cat.

Vocabulary:

- to climb   escalar
- to go up   subir
- to come down   bajar
- to try   intentar
- to ask   pedir
- polite   educado

12 Terrible danger

Adam **listened** to the story, but he didn't like it. It was scary.

The teacher showed the children a picture of Goldilocks. She was a very small girl. Then the teacher showed them a picture of the three bears. Baby Bear was quite cute, but Mother Bear was enormous and Father Bear was the biggest bear **ever**.

Adam knew Goldilocks was in **terrible** danger. **If** the bears came home and found Goldilocks in their house, they would **probably** eat her. If she tried to run away, they would chase her and catch her. **Then** they would eat her.

When the teacher read that Goldilocks climbed onto Baby Bear's bed and went to sleep, Adam **jumped up** and **shouted**: "Don't go to sleep, Goldilocks! **Run away**! The bears are coming!" The teacher looked at Adam and told him to sit down and be quiet.

Father Bear didn't eat Goldilocks. But he very nearly did, thought Adam.

Questions:
1. Which bear was the biggest?
2. What did Baby Bear look like?
3. What was the most dangerous thing Goldilocks did?

Vocabulary:

- to listen   escuchar
- ever   de la historia
- if   si
- probably   probablemente
- then   entonces
- to jump up   saltar
- to shout   gritar
- Run away!   ¡Huye!

13 Dogs can't climb trees

Do you know what I **decided** to do?

Dogs can't climb trees. That was the problem. Dogs can't climb trees, but cats can. So the white cat was in the tree, and I was under the tree. The cat was safe. Or was she?

It was simple, really.

Most cats are my **enemies**. But one is my friend. That's right – Zigzag is my friend, my family.

I jumped back over the fence into my garden and looked for Zigzag. He was where he **usually** is. He was on the sofa in the living room, sleeping.

I bit his tail just a little bit, to wake him up. He wasn't happy. He **hissed** at me.

I **explained** my problem with the white cat.

"Please help me, Zigzag," I said.

"Okay," said Zigzag. "But only if you **give** me what I want".

Maybe he's more intelligent than I thought.

Vocabulary:
- to decide   decidir
- most   la mayoría de
- enemy   enemigo
- usually   normalmente
- to hiss   sisear
- to explain   explicar
- to give   dar

14 The school rules

After the story, Adam's class went into the school **hall** - the biggest room in the school. All the other children in the school were already there, sitting on the floor.

The Headteacher **welcomed** the new children in Adam's class to the school. Then everyone **stood up** and sang a **song**. Adam didn't **know** what to sing, but he tried to **copy** the others.

After that, the Headteacher read the school **rules**:
1. Get to school on time.
2. Listen to the teacher.
3. Put your hand up if you want to ask a question.
4. Always **try hard**.
5. Don't **waste time**.
6. Be **kind** and polite.

Adam was **worried**. He wanted to ask a question, but he was too scared to put his hand up.

If a child broke a rule, was there a **punishment**?

Questions:
1. *What was the biggest room in the school called?*
2. *Which school rule do you think is the most important?*
3. *If you break a school rule at your school, is there a punishment?*

Vocabulary:

• hall	sala
• to welcome	dar la bienvenida
• to stand up	levantarse
• song	canción
• to know	saber
• to copy	copiar
• rule	regla
• to try hard	esforzarse
• to waste time	perder el tiempo
• kind	amable
• worried	preocupado
• punishment	castigo

15 The plan

This was the plan. It wasn't **difficult**. In fact, I thought it was very easy.

Zigzag is much bigger than the white cat. He just had to climb the tree and chase the white cat down to me. Simple.

But first, I had to do something for Zigzag.

Poor Zigzag. Because he's just a cat, he can't do much. He can't open the kitchen door. He can't open the fridge door. He can't take the cat food out of the fridge.

Zigzag hates waiting for dinner time. So he **often** asks me to give him his cat food. I **always** say no. Zigzag eats too much. **More** food isn't good for him.

But I really, really wanted that white cat. So, just this **once**, I opened the kitchen door and opened the fridge door. I took the cat food out of the fridge.

Zigzag ate some cat food. "I'm tired now," he said. "I want to go to sleep on my sofa".

"Oh no." I said. "Now you have to do what *I* want. Climb that tree!"

Vocabulary:
- difficult   difícil
- often   a menudo
- always   siempre
- more   más
- once   una vez

16 Lunch

Adam was hungry. When he went to nursery, he had a snack at eleven o'clock every morning. Today, he had to wait **until** lunchtime at half past twelve.

He played with **sand** and water and balls. He painted a picture of his cat and dog. He looked at the picture books in the big bookcase. He tried to write his name with a **pencil**.

And at last it was lunchtime. Some children had **packed lunches** from home in beautiful **lunchboxes**. They ate their sandwiches outside in the **playground.** But Adam went to the big hall again. This time, it was **full** of tables and chairs. He **queued** up for his food and sat down at a table next to a boy from his class. Lunch was chicken with **mashed potato** and **peas**. With strawberry ice cream for **pudding**. It wasn't delicious, but it wasn't too bad.

After lunch, Adam and his new friend ran outside. Adam saw Poppy playing football with the **older** boys and girls. He started to **enjoy** school.

Questions:
1. What was the most fun thing that Adam did?
2. What do you think of Adam's school lunch? Was it like your school lunches?

Vocabulary:
- until   hasta
- sand   arena
- pencil   lápiz
- packed lunch   almuerzo empacado
- lunchbox   fiambrera
- playground   patio de la escuela
- full   lleno
- to queue   hacer cola
- mashed potato   puré de patatas
- pea   guisante
- pudding   postre
- older   mayor
- to enjoy   disfrutar de

17 A lazy cat

Zigzag wasn't happy. He's a lazy cat. To be honest, he's an extremely lazy cat. He never wants to help people. He never wants to help other animals. He only thinks about himself. It's not really his fault. He's just a cat.

He walked into the garden. Very slowly. He jumped onto the garden fence. He jumped down into the neighbour's garden. He looked up at the tree. The white cat looked down at him. She stayed exactly where she was.

Then Zigzag ran at the tree. He jumped. And he fell. He fell back down. Zigzag is a big cat. He's a fat cat. I don't think he's very good at climbing trees.

Zigzag looked at me. "You ate the cat food." I said. "Now climb the tree!" Zigzag tried again. This time he **made it**. He was in the tree. But where was the white cat?

Vocabulary:
- to make it   llegar

18 Animal tracks

Look out for animal tracks in your garden or park. You can find them in snow or mud.

DOG   CAT

Watch out for bears – they're dangerous!

19 Bad dog!

The white cat was at the **top** of the tree. She was at the end of a thin **branch**.

"Go on, Zigzag! Chase that cat down!"

Zigzag slowly climbed up the tree. He climbed higher and higher. He climbed onto the white cat's branch. He was **almost** there.

CRACK!!

The branch broke. Zigzag fell down. The white cat fell down. I saw her and she saw me. She ran and I ran. I chased that cat round the garden. I chased her round the garden again. I chased her onto the **street**. I chased her down the street.

"Pam! **Stop!** Bad dog!"

Adam? Adam and Poppy and Mum? Back from school already? Where's the white cat? Oh no. She's up **another** tree. I WANT THAT CAT!

"Oh Pam", said Adam. "I had such a great time at school today."

Vocabulary:
- top   cima
- branch   rama
- almost   casi
- street   calle
- Stop!   ¡Para!
- another   otro

Find the opposites.

up	go
never	in
bad	different
the same	wake up
out	noisy
stop	dangerous
quiet	down
easy	good
cute	always
safe	scary
go to sleep	difficult

What are the words?

Adam is alm-st five. He's very y-ung, but he's a pol-t- child. He al-ays says thank you.

My dad says English is quite e-sy. But I'm ter-ibl- at it!

Your English is b-t-er than my English.

Please read me the -tor- of Goldilocks and the Three Bears. – In a m-n-te!

Respuestas:

6

1. She's four years older than Adam.
2. He felt excited, scared and a little bit proud. He really wanted to go to school.
3. Because his school uniform was red.

8

1. Because it was his first day at school.
2. No, he wasn't happy. He didn't want his mum to leave.
3. Because he didn't like him.

10

1. She went into the forest to find some breakfast.
2. No, they weren't; they were out.
3. No, he didn't want to eat her. He wanted to play with her.

12

1. Father Bear was the biggest.
2. He looked quite cute.
3. The most dangerous thing she did was to go to sleep on Baby Bear's bed.

14

1. It was called the school hall.
2. You decide.

16

1. You decide.
2. You decide.

up	down
never	always
bad	good
the same	different
out	in
stop	go
quiet	noisy
easy	difficult
cute	scary
safe	dangerous
go to sleep	wake up

Adam is almost five. He's very young, but he's a polite child. He always says thank you.

My dad says English is quite easy. But I'm terrible at it!

Your English is better than my English.

Please read me the story of Goldilocks and the Three Bears. – In a minute!

Gracias por leer este libro.

Póngase en contacto con nosotros:

Esperamos que usted y su hijo hayan encontrado este libro útil.

Si tiene alguna pregunta sobre este libro, envíenosla y nos pondremos en contacto con usted lo antes posible. Si tiene alguna sugerencia para la próxima edición de este libro, o para otros libros que le gustaría que publicáramos para ayudar a su hijo a aprender inglés, nos encantaría escucharla.

Escríbanos a: lydiawinter.zigzagenglish@gmail.com

Sitio web:

Puede echar un vistazo a nuestros otros libros para niños y adultos, jugar a algunos juegos en inglés y leer nuestro blog, en: **www.zigzagenglish.co.uk**.

Por favor...

...escribe una reseña sobre este libro. Las reseñas son importantes para otros padres y también para nosotros. Gracias.

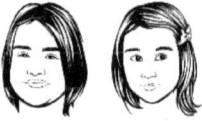

8A: A week's holiday

Katie: It's my **half term** holiday next week. A **whole** week with no school!

Anna: Are you going **away**?

Katie: Yes. We're going to the Lake District.

Anna: What's that? Where is it?

Katie: It's in the **north** of England. There are lots of **mountains** and **lakes**. It's very beautiful.

Anna: Lucky you! I have school next week.

Katie: School is really hard at the moment. I'm tired. I need a **break**.

Anna: Is your whole family going?

Katie: No. My mum has to work next week. So she's **staying** at home.

Anna: Your **poor** mum.

14. Present

The day after the last day of school was the first day of the summer holidays. But Ben didn't feel excited. He felt unhappy.

He **lay** on his bed in his bedroom with a book. But he didn't read the book. He thought about all those years at primary school. He thought about his friends.

His mum **called** him. "It's lunchtime, Ben! Come downstairs!"

Ben **sighed**. He went downstairs to the dining room. He **started** to say: "I'm not hungry, mum. I don't want any lunch." But then he stopped. What was that on the table? It was a **parcel**. Was it a **present**? For him?

CATEGORIES

WRITE DOWN 3:

1. School subjects

2. Small pets

3. Nice things to eat

4. Languages

5. Books in English

6. Annoying things children in your class do

7. Sea animals

8. English songs

9. Plants

10. Horrible things to eat

11. Funny people

12. Nice things to do on holiday

13. Jobs you don't want to do when you grow up

14. Long English words

15. Sports

16. Vegetables

17. Things your parents can do that you can't do

18. Short English words

19. Countries

20. American movies

www.ingramcontent.com/pod-product-compliance
Lightning Source LLC
LaVergne TN
LVHW051205080426
835508LV00021B/2816